Labor Unions in the United States

Labor Unions in the United States

←— A FIRST BOOK —→

by Carolyn Sims

illustrated with prints and photographs

FRANKLIN WATTS, INC.

845 Third Avenue, New York, N.Y. 10022

The author and publisher wish to acknowledge the assistance of Francis B. Conrad in the preparation of this book.

52112

SBN 531-00748-0
Copyright © 1971 by Franklin Watts, Inc.
Library of Congress Catalog Card Number: 72-172449
Printed in the United States of America
1 2 3 4 5

82- 14526

Contents

To Homeroom 231

Labor Unions in the United States

Why Do Men Band Together?

The basic idea that created labor unions is a simple one: there is strength in unity. When businesses were small, an individual employee could make arrangements with his employer about such issues as wages, hours, and job conditions. In time, as the United States became more industrialized and businesses grew, the average employee could no longer deal effectively with his employer. Workers began joining together so that they could deal with their employers as equals. This led to the creation of unions.

What the workers wanted can perhaps best be expressed in the first verse and chorus of "Solidarity Forever," the song that has become the anthem of the labor movement in America. Its message is:

> When the union's inspiration through the workers' blood shall
> run,

Labor Day parades are held every year to honor the working people in the United States. (Local 23-25 ILGWU)

There can be no power greater anywhere beneath the sun.
Yet what force on earth is weaker than the feeble strength of
    one?
But the union makes us strong.
Chorus: Solidarity forever!
         Solidarity forever!
         Solidarity forever!
         For the union makes us strong.

The strength of the local union is felt even in politics. Here, in a re-election bid by former New York City Mayor Robert Wagner, an appeal for votes is made to members of a local union. (Local 23-25 ILGWU)

How Unions
Are Organized

The Local Union

The American labor union movement altered its nature to fit changing times. What is true of union organization today may very well be different tomorrow as the needs of union members change.

Although there are certain things common to all union organization, it is important to remember that many statements do not apply to all unions. One thing that has always been true of unions and probably always will be is that the strength of any labor organization is found in the individual worker and his role as a member of a local union. Though national unions and their federations may gain most of the attention, a union stands or falls on how it acts to and for its individual local member.

A typical local union may be made up of workers in a single occupation, such as tugboat captains or airline pilots. Usually,

Workers report for a meeting in Washington, D.C. (AFL-CIO)

however, a local union consists entirely of workers employed in a single factory or business, such as automobile workers in one plant or clerks in one store.

At present, there are more than seventy thousand local unions in the United States. The size of these locals varies greatly. Although the exact structure of a local union varies, some general features are almost the same all over the United States.

A local union usually has a written constitution and bylaws that govern its membership, its purpose, its organization, and its methods of achieving its objectives.

The officers of most local unions are elected for a period of one to three years. They are usually the same as those in most clubs

8

or organizations: a president, one or more vice-presidents, a secretary, and a treasurer. In most small locals, the officers are employed full time on their regular jobs and carry on their union work, without pay, in their spare time. Many small locals, however, have at least one paid worker, usually called a *business agent,* who draws a salary directly from union dues and works full time on behalf of the members. Large locals have full-time staffs, with officers paid by the union.

Direct relations between the local and its members are handled by shop stewards. They are generally workers actually on the job, who are chosen by their fellow union members. They handle individual complaints and maintain daily contact with the union from an on-the-job level. Usually, each department in a factory or business, or each job area in a city-wide local, has at least one steward who represents the workers. In addition to the elected officers, shop stewards, and staff, individual members volunteer to serve as chairmen and members on the various committees that deal directly with management and the workers.

In many areas there are boards or councils that coordinate a number of locals in one area. The councils settle difficult problems that come up each day in the many areas where there are a large number of unions.

A common union problem concerns *jurisdiction.* Disputes over jurisdiction are concerned with determining what work will be performed by which types of skilled workers. Therefore, they affect the unions to which workers belong.

Here is an imaginary situation. Suppose a worker's job is to repair the brick oven in a bakery located in the cafeteria of an

In the nation's capital, the Smithsonian Institution signs its first contract with the Building Service Employees in 1965. (AFL-CIO)

automobile plant. Should he join the bricklayers' union because he works with bricks? Should he join the bakery workers' union because he works in a bakery? Or should he join the automobile workers' union because he works in an automobile factory? Because a union gains strength from the number of its members, each of these three unions would want him. A question like this affects both local and national unions. It may therefore be referred to the National Labor Relations Board, about which you will read more later, or to an industry-union group, such as the National Joint Board for Jurisdictional Disputes.

Although most locals are affiliated with a national union, some are not. Generally, the independent union is created within a single establishment to meet specific needs. Its members may feel there is little need to belong to a national organization since their goals are specialized.

Most local unions, however, find it beneficial to band together in a national union.

The National Union

National unions are comprised of all the individual locals in one craft or industry. This might mean all the union locals of electricians regardless of what kind of concern the members work in. It might be all the local unions of automobile workers regardless of what job each man does in an automobile plant. Like the locals, national unions vary widely in size. Today, there are over twenty national unions of less than a thousand members each. Yet the national unions of teamsters, automobile workers, and steelworkers each has well over a million members.

The most important governing body in a national union is the union convention. These conventions are held either annually or once every two years. Delegates from each local union that belongs to the national union attend the conventions. They elect the national officers and settle the most important questions of general policy, often only after long and heated debates and emotionally charged speeches.

Between conventions, the affairs of the national union are run by the elected officers and the staffs they choose. The national headquarters and offices for elected officials and paid staff members of

11

many unions are located in Washington, D.C. Representatives from the national headquarters travel all over the country to help and advise district councils and local unions. Often, the national union will bargain with a large employer on behalf of the national's locals instead of having each local bargain separately. The local depends on the officers and staff of its national union to help organize new workers, to give strike aid, to provide lawyers, accountants, economists, and other experts to solve local problems, and to settle major questions of jurisdiction with other national unions. In addition, the local relies on the national to deal with state and federal government agencies and to suggest or oppose legislation in the United States Congress.

Many broad questions of union policy cannot be put aside until a national convention can be held or a vote of all the union members can be taken. Therefore, the national officers and staff of a union usually exercise a great deal of power over the locals. Though the vast majority of national officers exercise this power with careful thought and restraint, there have been cases where the national officers have acted almost as dictators over their locals. Fortunately, federal and state legislation, public opinion, and the growing interest of local members in national affairs usually serve to prevent officers from taking permanent or excessive control over a local union.

Union Federation

Some national unions feel that it is best to be part of a federation that would represent all unions. At present, the American Federation of Labor-Congress of Industrial Organizations (AFL-CIO) consists of representatives of every member union. Today, there are over 120 national unions that belong to the federation, representing almost 16 million members. Although most of the membership belongs to national organizations, more than two hundred local unions with no national affiliation have chosen to be part of the AFL-CIO.

Some local and national unions are not associated with the AFL-CIO. There are more than thirteen thousand unaffiliated unions, including the largest national in the country, the Teamsters. Recently the giant United Auto Workers (UAW) withdrew from the AFL-CIO. These two unions have joined together to create the Alliance for Labor Action.

Federation has made labor powerful. Policies are centralized and in theory the federation guides all unions — local and national — to common goals that would benefit all labor. It serves the unions as an information and guidance agency. It may help member unions to conduct their financial and jurisdictional affairs. In addition, it often tries to set policies of equal opportunities for jobs for all.

World Labor Organization

Attempts have been made to persuade labor to support world organizations that would work for better conditions for all workers. As a result of disagreement about policies the United States has had an unstable history of membership and participation in any such movement.

13

The International Labor Organization (ILO), created in 1919, is the only world organization in which the United States has been an active member. It represents 117 countries. The ILO seeks to raise labor standards by making universal policies for the benefit of labor, by gathering and sharing information, and by giving technical guidance or assistance, especially to newly independent countries.

Panelists from the United States and Canada prepare for a conference on collective bargaining, sponsored by the AFL-CIO and the Canadian Labor Congress. (AFL-CIO)

Union Goals

Achieving workers' goals is the responsibility of union leaders. They speak to the employers or their representatives for all the members of the union. The job of the union leader in the United States is to secure a *contract* (a written legal agreement) that provides the greatest number of benefits possible for the union members and security for the union. The process of meeting for discussions with an employer or group of employers is known as *collective bargaining*. The result of collective bargaining is the contract, which will determine the relations between labor and management for a specified time. The relationship between workers and management, or employer and employee, is often called labor-management relations.

Collective bargaining deals with six basic areas: wages, job security, hours of work, working conditions, fringe benefits, and grievance procedures. We can best understand what union members want to accomplish by examining each of these areas.

15

When a contract is finally approved, all parties must sign it. This is a formal occasion. (USWA)

The collective bargaining table. (AFL-CIO)

Wages

There are many wage questions for the union leaders and employers to settle. First, the bargainers must describe each job accurately to ensure a standard rate of pay for a specific job. After the duties of each type of work have been made clear, the amount of money to be paid per hour, day, or week is debated. Of course, the union wants each worker to be as highly paid as possible, while the employer tries to keep the wages at a rate that allows him to make what he considers a fair profit without having to overprice his products. Once the regular wages have been determined, extra pay for such special situations as night and overtime work, Saturday and holiday work, and working under hazardous conditions is discussed until both sides agree.

Job Security

One of the most important reasons for joining a union is to gain job security. Before unions existed, workers could be fired at any time and for any reason. A worker could be laid off, or told not to come into work until further notification, with no explanation from the employer.

The reasons for firing a worker were often unrelated to the way he did his job. If he displeased the employer by complaining, or even if he wore clothes his employer did not like, the worker could be fired or laid off — even if he was the best worker the employer had. When labor unions were first being organized, a worker often was fired on the spot if his employer thought he belonged to a union.

If business was slow and the employer did not need all his workers, he would often decide who to lay off and who to keep on the basis of friendship, religion, race, or age.

The union's job has been to make certain that no worker can be fired without good cause. Under a union contract, when a worker or workers must be laid off, the employees who stay are usually those who have been with the company for the longest period of time.

Hours of Work

The standard length of a work week varies, but today, it is usually forty hours. Though the total number of working hours is established almost by custom, the union and the employer must bargain over when the day begins, when it ends, and which days are working ones.

With a set number of hours to be worked, each employee knows what is expected and each employer knows what to expect. If a worker does work beyond his regular hours, he is working *overtime,* that is, over his regular time, and he must be paid accordingly.

Arrangements must be made to determine when an employee is actually considered to be at work. For example: Does a working day begin when the employee enters the front gate of the factory, or when he walks into the plant itself, or only when he actually reaches his working position? Can a worker wash up on the time he is being paid for or must he do so on his own time? These are important questions to workers in a factory.

18

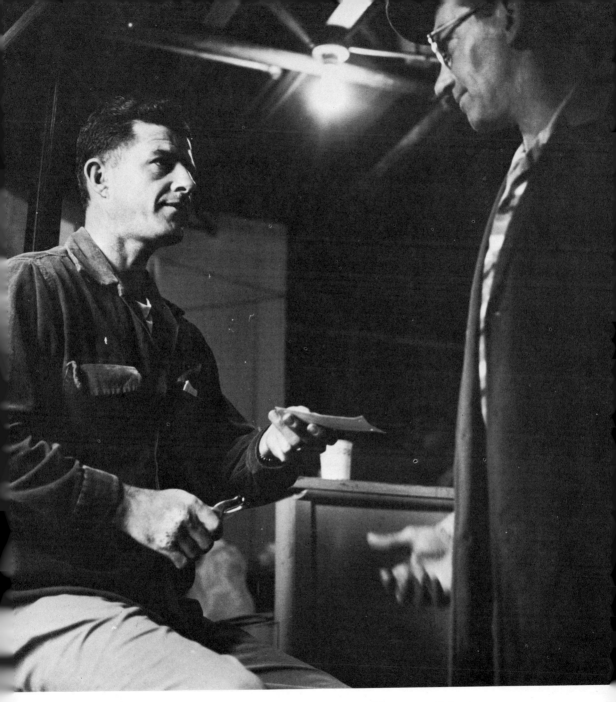

Workers check in and out of their places of work, making sure their time cards are punched. In most cases this is done by machine. (USWA)

Fringe benefits are important to the worker. Here, steelworkers prepare to strike over pensions and insurance. (USWA)

Working Conditions

While the union and the employer bargain on the major issues of wages, job security, and hours, they also bargain about questions concerning working conditions. Naturally, proper working conditions differ from industry to industry, business to business, and job to job. Many jobs involve special difficulties or dangers and it is usually the task of the union to make sure the employer recognizes and tries to correct or make allowances for these problems. The union presents the workers' demands for proper lighting and ventilation, rest periods, and coffee breaks. Perhaps most important, the union makes sure the employers' demands for work output are fair under the existing conditions. Each of these questions must be settled separately in the bargaining that takes place between the union and the employer.

Fringe Benefits

As wages increase, hours shorten, security becomes stronger, and conditions of the job improve, the fringe benefits become more important in labor-management agreements. They include vacation time and pay; sick leave, or pay when a worker is ill; paid holidays; severance pay, or pay that is given to the worker if he is let go; pay for the times when the worker must serve on jury duty; the benefits of hospitalization, medical insurance, and life insurance; and pensions and retirement plans. Arrangements also must be settled for the handling of the status of the worker leaving for military service, or for maternity leave.

Practicality

Since a contract is usually long and complex, and is often in effect for as long as three years, a number of problems are certain to come up under the agreement. It would be unfair to make either the employer or the employee wait for perhaps months or years until the contract expires to have these problems settled. Instead, the contract itself contains the actual method for settling special problems as they arise.

A grievance is a wrong, real or imagined, that is considered a ground for complaint. A procedure is the means that the employees and the employers work out to air these complaints. Therefore, a grievance procedure is the machinery used to present a complaint. This is important to unions, because grievances involve difficulties encountered by workers on a day-to-day basis.

How the Union Works to Achieve Its Goals

Collective bargaining can take place at any level: between local and company, local and factory, national and industry representatives. To see how collective bargaining works, we will trace the procedures through the negotiations between a local and a company.

Collective Bargaining

Although actual bargaining for a new contract takes place only toward the end of an agreement, the process related to this actual bargaining goes on continuously. While a contract is in effect, both the union and management carefully watch to see how the terms of the agreement are working. Bargaining for a new contract is a long and complex procedure. First, usually sixty days before an existing contract is due to expire, the union local notifies the company of its plans to revise the old agreement.

23

Negotiating sessions are often long. Some of the men here have begun to make themselves comfortable for the hours ahead. (USWA)

The union researches the financial position of the company. If the local belongs to a national union, the national supplies facts and experts to suggest terms for a new contract. The shop stewards ask the men for suggestions about the new agreement.

Finally, the union bargaining committee, in cooperation with the local officers, compiles a list of changes and demands it wants included. The original list often demands more than what the union is willing to settle for so that the bargaining committee can compromise between union demands and company offers.

The real bargaining or negotiating begins when company and union representatives meet. The union negotiating committee consists of members of the union bargaining committee who, with local officers, have prepared the union's position. The company is usually represented by its factory manager, its industrial relations manager, and lawyers. If a business or factory is small, the owner or factory manager often attends the bargaining sessions. The first few meetings are usually devoted to general statements; they also allow both sides to acquaint themselves with the personalities and ideas of the opposition.

During the bargaining, each side presents its demands and counteroffers or counterproposals. Naturally, certain points are more important to the union than are others. In normal bargaining procedure, minor issues are settled before bargaining begins over the most important ones.

As the bargaining goes on, it is customary for the union to reduce its demands gradually, while the company gradually increases its offers. This practice is similar to what takes place when a buyer and a seller argue over the price of an item in a marketplace. Sometimes the union and the company will call in a neutral third party to examine the positions. The job of the third party — whether it be called an arbitrator, a conciliator, or a fact-finding board — is to help bring about an agreement.

When the union negotiating committee and the company representatives finally agree, the job is not over. Before the new contract can go into effect, usually the entire union membership must vote to accept or reject it. If the union members do not agree with the proposed contract and the past contract has expired, they can vote in favor of further negotiations, or they can vote to strike until the company meets their original demands. The vast majority of contracts, however, are negotiated without a strike. Simple bargaining in good faith by both sides has proved to be the best way to settle labor disputes.

A union meeting at Madison Square Garden in New York is called so that members can vote on whether to strike. (AFL-CIO)

The Strike

A strike is defined by the United States Bureau of Labor Statistics as "a temporary stoppage of work by a group of employees . . . to express a grievance or to enforce a demand."

There are different kinds of strikes. During a sit-down strike the workers remain at their jobs but refuse to work. The sit-down tactic is rarely used today, but it once was an effective action against employers.

Another kind of strike is the slow-down strike, where workers continue to work, but not as hard as they usually do. This is particularly effective in a factory, where the workers' output can be easily measured.

Recently, particularly among public employees, a new kind of union tactic has emerged — the *job action*. Here, men and women report to work but refuse to do certain aspects of their jobs. In this way, such people as doctors, nurses, policemen, and firemen stop just short of bringing on the total disaster that would result from a complete work stoppage. For example, in 1971, during a dispute over wages, patrolmen in New York City reported to their local precincts but refused to walk their beats.

During the third and most commonly used kind of strike, workers do not report to their jobs at all. Under such circumstances the workers agree not to come to work until an agreement is reached over a specific issue. In this way, pressure is exerted on the employer, who usually cannot afford to lose business and will therefore listen and reason with the employees and their representatives. On the other hand, when an employee is on strike he is not paid. Strik-

27

*A strike by a local union
over unfair treatment of workers
brought these two women
out to picket.
(Local 23-25* ILGWU*)*

ing is the last resort for the worker and at the same time it is his most important weapon.

When a stalemate is reached in collective bargaining, the decision to strike is determined by a union vote. At this point, the union members will almost always vote in favor of the strike. Even the threat of a strike will often help them in the bargaining negotiations.

The officers of the union set the time and date for the strike to begin, and when the moment is reached, the workers leave the job. When workers are out on strike, they *picket* — march or walk around the factory or business — usually carrying signs that express their complaints. Before the strike begins, the local strike committee assigns each worker certain time on the picket line so each will serve his fair share.

The picket line serves to inform the public about union problems and it also attempts to prevent all employees from reporting to work. To work when a strike is on is called *crossing a picket line.* Often, these picket lines also serve to discourage customers from entering a place of business, or suppliers from making deliveries or pickups, thereby further decreasing the employers' business. This places an additional pressure on the employer to come to an agreement with the union.

The strike committee sees to it that the workers receive food and money from the union. Not all unions have such strike benefits, but as union membership becomes increasingly stable, more unions have an opportunity to build up their treasury so they can help their members while they are not receiving their full pay.

Though some strikes go on for weeks or even months, most last only a few days.

When an agreement is finally reached and the members vote to accept it, the workers return to their jobs and the strike is over.

Grievance Machinery

Not all problems are solved by collective bargaining. In fact, one of the goals of the bargaining is to establish the means by which an employee can express a complaint about his work or working conditions and receive a fair hearing from management, without jeopardizing his job. Both the process and the specific conditions under which grievance machinery can actually be used are defined in the contract. Here is an example of the way it might work.

A contract is signed: the strike is over. (AFL-CIO)

Local 100 of a national union had about four hundred members, all of whom worked at the CC Products Company, a small factory that made U-bolts and muffler clamps, which are used on cars and trucks.

One day, two things happened. The company installed a new kind of stamping machinery that bent the steel bolts into a U-shape and was designed to increase production. On the same day, the company canceled its contract with a firm whose mobile wagons allowed workers to order coffee at their workplaces. Instead of the wagons, the company installed coffee machines at one location in the factory.

John Johnson, a CC employee and a member of Local 100, worked at the large stamping machine. When the new machine was installed, the foreman told John that he would now be expected to bend about six hundred bolts a day instead of the four hundred he had bent on the old machine. As John tried to increase his production, he found that he could not do the job properly. To add to his troubles, the long trip to the coffee machines cut into his coffee break.

Finally, John went to see Bill Smith, his shop steward — the union representative for John's area. They discussed the new stamping machine and the higher quota. At the same time, John mentioned that the coffee machines allowed him only five minutes for his break, not the supposed fifteen. Bill agreed that John had a complaint on both counts. Since a number of other workers had been complaining about the inconvenience of the coffee machines, the shop steward decided to tackle that problem first.

He knew that under the CC company contract, like under most union contracts, a complaint cannot be a grievance unless it is related to some part of that agreement between the company and the local union. So the first step was to read the contract. He found that the company had agreed to provide an opportunity each morning for every worker to purchase coffee "at a convenient point that will allow the worker fifteen minutes to drink his coffee." Next Bill went to the plant foreman and they discussed the problem. Bill pointed out that the new machines were not convenient to most of the workers and that this was in violation of the contract.

The plant foreman saw Bill's point and went to the plant manager in the executive office. He returned a short while later with news. The manager agreed to take out the coffee machines and to have the mobile coffee wagons returned.

Most grievances are settled in this manner. In larger factories, the usual rule is that all grievances must be presented in writing before they can be acted upon. However, small grievances can usually be handled by an informal discussion between the foreman and the shop steward.

Although a simple conference cleared up the first matter, the problem of work standards on the new machine installed for John Johnson remained. When John first spoke to Bill Smith, the steward suggested that John continue working a few more days on the new machine until he was familiar with it. If John still felt that the foreman was asking him to turn out more than a normal person working at a normal pace could produce, then John could renew his grievance. John felt this was fair and agreed to give the new machine a longer trial. However, after a week, John found that he could bend only about five hundred bolts a day, no matter how hard he tried.

John went to Bill once more. Bill watched John work and felt that John could not bend more than five hundred bolts a day without overtaxing himself. Bill found that the contract stated that "a worker will be called on to do no more than a reasonable amount of work each day and the company will not make unreasonable demands upon a worker's time or strength."

As shop steward for the union, Bill Smith had seen many cases of this type before. He knew that the question of whether John's complaint was a proper grievance depended on what the words "reasonable" and "unreasonable" really meant. The company evidently thought that six hundred bolts a day was a "reasonable" request, while John Johnson felt that any amount over five hundred was "unreasonable." Bill knew that this was not a simple grievance that could be solved by an informal chat between himself and the foreman so he started the grievance machinery in operation by writing out a formal grievance report. In this report, Bill presented the facts of the case as he and John saw them.

When the report was finished, Bill gave a copy to the foreman with a request that the foreman tell John Johnson that he should not have to bend more than five hundred bolts a day. The foreman explained that the company would have to decide how much work John should produce. Bill and the foreman agreed that this grievance would have to be taken up by the factory grievance committee. The foreman wrote out his own report of the situation. Bill's and the foreman's reports were turned over to a grievance committee, made up of employees and union representatives. It met with management once every two weeks to discuss the various grievances that the shop stewards and foreman had not been able to settle on their own.

When the grievance committee took up John's grievance, they found they could not agree with management on a solution. The committee agreed with John and Bill that five hundred bolts was a "reasonable" amount. The management thought that six hundred was not "unreasonable."

When both sides saw they could not agree, they took what is usually the final step in grievance machinery: they called in an arbitrator. An arbitrator usually is chosen from a list given to the union and the management by the American Arbitration Association, the Federal Mediation and Conciliation Service, or state mediation agencies. In John's case, the arbitrator was an economics professor from a local college whom the union and the company had agreed to use in cases where the grievance committee could not settle a problem among themselves.

In most cases, the union and the company each pay half of the arbitrator's fee, usually about $150 per day. It normally takes about a day to listen to each side of a grievance on the local level and to determine the facts. Because the arbitrator's decision may not resolve the issue in a manner acceptable to both sides, many problems are ended only temporarily by arbitration. When the time comes for the union and the company to discuss a new contract, one side or the other will often bring up old grievances as matters for bargaining. In John Johnson's case, the arbitrator decided that 520 bolts a day was a "reasonable" number to ask John to bend. Because the union and the company had agreed in advance to accept the arbitrator's decision, the disagreement stopped there. However, when it comes time for a new contract, the issue of defining a "reasonable" amount of work may arise.

In his daily work, a typical union member most often sees his local operating on his behalf through the grievance machinery.

A Brief History of the American Labor Movement

The history of the American labor movement is really the history of the growth of union membership. It began with local unions that realized they could not effect new reforms unless they banded together at a national level. As businesses merged into increasingly larger companies, it became apparent that the national unions, too, would have to merge into federations to become a strong power at the collective bargaining table. The balance of power that resulted is what exists today. But it was not always this way.

The Early Years

Late in the eighteenth century, skilled craftsmen, such as shoemakers, printers, and carpenters, formed into small, separate groups in large cities and organized the first real unions in the United

States. They were fighting the lowering of their wages. These unions were very weak and had small memberships because a worker feared he would be fired if his employer found out that he belonged to one. Furthermore, once a specific issue was settled, members lost interest, and the group disbanded.

Employers had two weapons against the early unions — they could fire workers who joined and they could turn to the courts for help. According to traditional English common law, unions were, in fact, "conspiracies in restraint of trade." The reasoning behind the law was that any combination of workers attempting to raise wages was an act directed against the public interest and was punishable by law. Therefore the unions were deprived of their very right to exist.

By 1820, only a small number of employees — the bravest — belonged to unions. Workers continued to seek ways to fight the overwhelming strength and power of their employers. Soon organizations of craft workers began to form once more in large cities. Although these unions were usually made up entirely of workers in one craft who lived in a single area, unions of general factory workers, or unskilled laborers, also began to appear.

During the 1820's and 1830's, these workers' organizations were turned from direct bargaining with employers to politics in order to gain benefits for their members. If individual employers would not give in to the workers, then the workers would elect public officials who had power to make laws that would help them.

In some eastern states, local labor parties and political councils began to nominate and often elect candidates to city and state offices. These candidates were usually pledged to support workers'

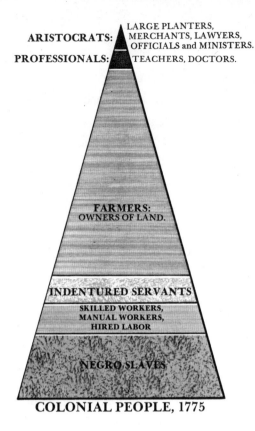

ARISTOCRATS: LARGE PLANTERS, MERCHANTS, LAWYERS, OFFICIALS and MINISTERS.

PROFESSIONALS: TEACHERS, DOCTORS.

FARMERS: OWNERS OF LAND.

INDENTURED SERVANTS

SKILLED WORKERS, MANUAL WORKERS, HIRED LABOR

NEGRO SLAVES

COLONIAL PEOPLE, 1775

Chart of population social pyramid

objectives to reform political and social ills. They called for restriction of child labor, free and equal public school education, the ending of imprisonment for debt, the establishment of a ten-hour day for all workers, and the elimination of home and factory sweatshops. In most sweatshops, workers were crowded together, underpaid, and compelled to work long hours under poor conditions. Although the local political organizations never gained much more than temporary power, they did call public attention to the plight of workers, and many state legislatures did enact laws for social reform.

37

Perhaps feeling that they had now gained enough political power to ensure the unions' success, American workers turned again to the idea of unions that would bargain directly for their members. In the 1830's, craft and factory workers in the East and Middle West began to organize. Until then union activity had existed only on a local basis, but now workers in such trades as typography, weaving, and carpentry established short-lived national organizations.

A major economic depression in the 1840's temporarily halted union growth. Workers were so badly in need of jobs that they would do nothing that might anger their employers — including joining a union. This setback, however, was only temporary, and by the 1850's most important trades had established some kind of union organization.

Once again unions were being established on a national level. In 1850, printers from all over the country gathered at a national union convention. Within ten years, hat finishers, metal molders, stonecutters, machinists, and locomotive engineers had also created national organizations. The movement, however, was only beginning, for none of the new organizations was truly effective.

The Civil War (1861–65) provided a powerful stimulus to the growth of the American labor movement. Because the war required large quantities of factory goods, profits and prices rose, and many new industries were founded. Naturally, unions did their best to organize at least the skilled factory workers. Whereas in 1863, there were about eighty local unions in twenty northern states; by 1864, the number of locals had grown to nearly three hundred. The new unions were strong and vital, and a few of them — such as brick-

This 1860 shoemakers' strike in Massachusetts was evidence of the growth of labor organizing. (LIBRARY OF CONGRESS)

layers, cigarmakers, and painters — still exist in only slightly different forms.

In 1866, the National Labor Union, the first really national labor organization, was formed in Baltimore. Its initial objective was an eight-hour day. The National Labor Union soon entered politics, however, and promoted cooperatives, which allowed the workers to own a business and share the profits. The National Labor Union lost its strength with its move into politics and it disbanded in 1872.

The Emergence of Modern Unions

An economic depression in the 1870's once more reduced the power of unions. Competition over jobs was sharp. Any job, no matter how long the hours, how poor the wages, and how terrible the working conditions, was better than none at all. And again workers feared that union membership would cost them their jobs.

However, at this same time, America was beginning to feel the effects of an industrial revolution. New factories were springing up, the assembly line was emerging as a factor in the economy, and, as a result, more workers than ever were needed. Now, for example, instead of one man — the cobbler — making a complete pair of shoes, many people, each with a specific job, would work on all the shoes. One might make the sole, another the heel, and another the last. And yet another person would put all the pieces together. Therefore, instead of skilled workers, all that was needed were people who could be taught to do the same thing over and over again, all day long.

Where was the labor force to come from? At this time, people from all over the world were landing on America's shores in search of new opportunities in a new land. Unable to speak English, they could work only where a knowledge of the language was not essential. So they eagerly turned to the factories. These people were willing to accept any wages, any hours, any working conditions. They found jobs not only on factory assembly lines, but in mines and on railroads as well. The situation simmered, building up the momentum to explode. All the workers were competing — the immigrant versus the native-born American, in many cases the black

40

*A Knights of Labor
convention late in the
nineteenth century.*
(LIBRARY OF CONGRESS)

American; the laborers working under poor conditions versus the
employer who took advantage of all these factors. Something had
to give. The time was ripe for labor to organize.

The year 1869 is often designated as the beginning of the
modern labor movement. In that year a small group of clothing
workers in Philadelphia founded a union called the Noble Order
of the Knights of Labor. Its first leader was Uriah Stephens. At
first it was a secret organization with rituals and codes, which ap-
pealed to workers who would not join a union that publicly
declared itself a union. The members gained confidence as membership increased, and finally they revealed themselves to the public. The Knights of Labor grew slowly but steadily, attracting

41

workers from other crafts and other parts of the country. Then, during the first years of the 1880's, the growth became much more rapid and membership rose from less than 10,000 in 1879 to over 700,000 in 1886. The main aim of the Knights was to replace existing businesses with a series of cooperatives that would give the workers the chance to profit from the products they made.

More practically, the Knights wanted an eight-hour day; public ownership of such utilities as gas, electric, and transportation companies; equal pay for women; and the abolition of convict labor, which allowed an employer to use free prison labor rather than paid employees. The Knights hoped to achieve their goals through political power and public education. They felt that strikes were to be used only as a last resort. However, local organizations that belonged to the Knights felt differently and, as a result, many strikes took place. But when one set of workers went on strike the employer could hire other workers to take their places. The strikers called the strikebreaking workers *scabs*. Strikers and scabs often clashed violently.

In time, the striking workers were even singing about the lowly scabs. To the tune of "The Worms Crawl In," strikers on picket lines all over the United States were heard singing:

The scabs crawl in, the scabs crawl out,
They crawl in under and all about.
They crawl in early, they crawl in late,
They crawl in under the factory gate.

The organization of a group called the Molly Maguires not

only added to the violence but also drew attention to unions and made the public think of them as violent. The Molly Maguires were not really a labor union but an active secret organization that became powerful in the Pennsylvania coal mines. It had no real goals but served to aggravate the already miserable conditions of the mine workers. Since they were the only active group aware of the horrible conditions, the miners responded to the Molly Maguires and looked to them as a possible means through which they could improve their lot. Unfortunately for the mine workers, the Molly Maguires were more interested in violence than in bargaining for better wages, hours, and working conditions. Eventually the group's leaders were jailed.

Management, meanwhile, was devising new weapons to use against the workers. An owner would close his factory or business rather than give in to the demands of his employees. This action was called a *lockout* because the workers were actually locked out of their jobs. Lockouts caused considerable hardship, because with no work there was no pay. In the future, the workers would be less inclined to strike.

Strikes at this time did little for the workers involved. They did focus public attention on a troubled area in a supposedly prospering country, but they also roused resentment.

The difficulties were aggravated by quarreling among the leadership of the Knights of Labor. The leaders disagreed over whether the organization was to be primarily a political or a labor group. Furthermore, the membership included craft workers, skilled workers, and unskilled workers — virtually anyone who wanted to belong.

The 1886 riot in Haymarket Square, Chicago, was a major setback for labor. There had long been tension between the city's workers and policemen. These tensions erupted at a meeting on May 4: a bomb was thrown, shots were fired there were fatalities among both workers and police. Eight men were tried and convicted of murdering a policeman. The accused were also tried for their supposedly revolutionary and anti-government ideas. The labor movement was seriously damaged in America's first big red scare. The greatest casualty, perhaps, was the issue of the eight-hour day. (BROWN BROTHERS)

Large craft unions, which might have added strength to the Knights, felt that their interests were different from the political and social interests of many of the Knights members and refused to join. Though the Knights remained in existence until 1917, their influence in the American labor union movement was over by 1890.

In 1881, six of the most important craft unions — the printers, cigarmakers, carpenters, glassworkers, metal molders, and iron- and steelworkers — and representatives of smaller labor organizations met in Pittsburgh to form the Federation of Organized Trades and Labor Unions (FOTLU) of the United States and Canada. There were about forty-five thousand members led by Samuel Gompers and Adolph Strasser, both of the cigarmakers union. During its first five years of existence, this new organization remained very weak in comparison with the powerful Knights of Labor.

Then, in 1886, some of the large craft unions belonging to the Knights of Labor disagreed with the policies of the parent union and held a separate meeting in Columbus, Ohio, to found the American Federation of Labor (AFL). The Federation of Organized Trades and Labor Unions happened to be meeting in Columbus at the same time and the two groups decided to unite. Samuel Gompers of the FOTLU was elected the first president of the new AFL, a job he held (except for one year) until he died in 1924.

By 1896, the ten-year-old AFL had almost 300,000 members. Gradually, it became the most important labor organization in the United States, with 1.5 million members in 1904, 2 million in 1914, and more than 4 million members in 1920 — about 80 percent of all union workers.

While the AFL was growing, attempts were made by some

English-born Samuel Gompers (1850–1924) was recognized as head of the American labor movement for nearly forty years. (AFL-CIO)

AFL leaders to turn the federation into a radical left organization. In 1905, the Industrial Workers of the World (IWW) was formed. With the aim of overthrowing capitalism, it resorted to violence and strikes. Although the AFL was trying to gain better working conditions for its members within the system, many people could not see the difference between its aims and the IWW's, and the labor movement as a whole again had to withstand unfavorable public opinion. The controversy continued until World War I, when the IWW simply dropped out of sight and most of its leaders disappeared.

Despite the peaceful aims of the AFL, labor struggles became more frequent and bitter as the unions grew more powerful. However, management had a weapon that was to hamper union growth

— the use of a court order called an *injunction,* which was issued to stop strikes. The injunction forced striking union members to go back to work or look for new jobs. Another weapon used by management was the *yellow-dog contract,* which was a piece of paper signed by the worker stating that he would not join a union. If the worker broke the contract, he was automatically fired. The courts ruled that this contract was legal. A third weapon of management was the hiring of scabs. This led to fights and bloodshed.

In 1892, members of the Amalgamated Association of Iron and Steel Workers were fighting for the rights of the workers at the Carnegie Steel Company at Homestead, Pennsylvania. The company hired detectives from the Pinkerton agency to break the strike. The violence between the strikers and the Pinkertons was so intense that the National Guard had to be called in to restore order.

Two years later, in 1894, Eugene Debs, leader of the American Railway Union, called a strike against the Pullman Palace Parlor Car Company in Illinois. Many railroad workers in the Chicago area walked out on their jobs in sympathy. The clash was bitter, and federal and state troops were again called to bring the workers back into line.

The struggle over the balance of power between labor and management made these incidents bitter and intense. Workers were determined to gain their rights even if they had to fight and be jailed. Management was equally determined to ignore the demands of the workers, and it had the support of the courts because the right of unions to exist had not been established legally. The turning point came with new legislation and new court interpretations of laws that would allow unions to exist and to represent their members.

47

Violence during the Homestead strike at the Carnegie Steel Company in Pennsylvania in 1892 brought death to ten people. Here, after the strikers surrendered, Pinkerton men leave the scene. (BROWN BROTHERS)

Fire at the Triangle Shirtwaist Company in New York City on March 25, 1911, made the public aware of inhuman working conditions and the need for safety regulations. Within thirty minutes, 146 workers were burned to death at their tables. (NEW YORK HISTORICAL SOCIETY)

Clauses in the Clayton Anti-Trust Act, passed in 1914, further improved the status of unions. Primarily, the act declared that a union was not a "conspiracy in restraint of trade" and therefore had the right to exist. Second, the use of the injunction to stop strikes was limited. The court's interpretation of the new law made the gains for unions short-lived, but under the act, unions were able to realize some of their practical goals.

The unions' first and most important objective was to gain recognition as representatives of the workers. They wanted to negotiate peaceful collective bargaining agreements, which would raise wages, secure better working conditions, and establish a standard eight-hour day.

In the first years of the twentieth century, the practicality of this program brought about legislation favorable to unions. Several states enacted laws regulating the use of women and child labor. Other laws established standards for working conditions. Most states passed workmen's compensation laws that provided for payment to workers injured on their jobs. During this time, the United States Congress established a separate Department of Labor to deal with the problems of the workers.

The rapid growth of industry during the First World War greatly benefited unions and union members. By 1920, there were over 5 million union members. Wages in the United States had risen. The average number of working hours fell from about sixty hours per week in 1890 to about forty-six hours a week in 1924.

After the war, the need for factory workers dropped. It was the old story. Wages fell. Membership in unions dropped: in 1920, 5 million members; in 1923, 3½ million members, and it stayed at this level until the early 1930's.

Although union membership did not increase during the twenties and early thirties, the national union movement gained two important victories that paved the way for its growth. First, the Railway Labor Act (1926) assured railroad workers of the right to organize and join unions without employer interference and under protection of the federal government. Even though this legislation was limited to railroad workers, it led to legislation that included workers in all industries.

Even more important was the Norris-LaGuardia Act (1932), which greatly limited the power of the federal courts in preventing strikes and picketing. Until then the courts had been able to issue injunctions requiring workers to work or lose their jobs. Now the courts could no longer use the injunction against the workers or the unions. This act also forbade the use of the yellow-dog contract: employees no longer had to swear to their employers that they would not join a union.

In 1935, Congress passed the National Labor Relations Act, more often referred to as the Wagner Act. It guaranteed workers "the right to self-organization, to form, join, or assist labor organizations, to bargain collectively through representatives of their own choosing, and to engage in concerted activities, for the purpose of collective bargaining or other mutual aid or protection." This actually meant that the national government would protect the rights of workers to form and join labor unions. In addition, these unions were recognized as the official representatives of the workers and could bargain with employers. This was the go-ahead for workers to organize.

As part of the Wagner Act, an administrative agency called the National Labor Relations Board (NLRB) was created to oversee and protect the rights of workers and unions. Of its many duties, two were most important. First, the board was to prevent employers from engaging in "unfair labor practices" that might interfere with the formation of labor unions or prevent their being effective after formation. Second, in exercising its power to determine worker representatives, or unions, the NLRB ensured the fairness through secret elections of deciding which union would represent a particular group of workers.

The importance of the Wagner Act to the growth of the membership of unions can be seen in one simple statistic: in 1935, when the act was passed, there were about 3,725,000 union members in the United States; by 1937, two years later, union membership nearly doubled to 7,225,000.

Most of the new union members were workers in large industries like automobile, rubber, and aluminum. Many were unskilled or semiskilled laborers who did not fit strictly into one craft or occupational category. As we have seen, traditional unionism in the United States had grown on a craft basis, and the established craft unions, which were the largest part of the AFL, did not know how to deal with hundreds of thousands of workers who did not have any certain occupation.

As the AFL unions began to expand in the 1930's, a struggle developed among the organization's leaders over whether workers should be organized on a craft- or industry-wide basis. Since the majority of AFL leaders voted in favor of only craft organizations, many workers in the large, mass-production industries, such as steel and automobile, were eliminated. A split developed in 1935 that was to last until 1955 and which continues to be an issue among some unions today. Shortly after the national AFL convention in 1935, officers of eight AFL unions decided to form a new union to organize workers on an industrial rather than a craft basis. The name chosen for this new organization was the Committee for Industrial Organization (CIO).

For three years, union leaders tried to keep this new organization connected with the AFL, but in November, 1938, the CIO held its first organizational convention and the break with the AFL was complete. John L. Lewis, president of the powerful United Mine Workers, was elected first president of the newly named Congress of Industrial Organization (CIO). The new union turned its efforts to organizing workers in industries that the AFL had been neglecting. The CIO's first efforts were directed to the steel, textile, and automobile industries, where unions had never before held any real power. The strong competition between the CIO and the AFL stimulated the growth of the union movement. By the end of 1942, there were about 11 million union members in the United States.

During this period, most union organization was accomplished with much less struggle than at any time in the past — although there were some difficult strikes especially in the automobile, steel, and rubber industries. The National Labor Relations Board protected the rights of the workers. In addition, employers were becoming increasingly aware that a responsible union acting in the best interests of its members helped get the most efficient and most profitable work from employees.

After World War II and New Laws

During World War II, the American economy expanded rapidly to meet the nation's tremendous needs for war materials. Union membership grew at an equally fast pace: at a rate of about one million additional new union members a year. Some unions — especially those involved in the metal trades — doubled or even tripled their membership. No one wanted to hurt the war effort, so there were few strikes during this period.

However, when the war ended in 1945, the United States was hit by a period of labor unrest. In wartime, overtime pay had been a major factor in increasing the take-home pay of workers. When the war ended, most unions sought a pay increase of about 30 percent for their members so that the elimination of overtime would not result in a pay cut. Many employers were afraid they could not meet the demands of the unions and make enough profit to remain in business. This difference of opinion between employers and unions led to a large number of strikes during the first year after the war ended. In the period between August, 1945, and July, 1946, there were over forty major strikes involving ten thousand or more workers each. The total number of strikes for that period reached over four thousand, involving almost 5 million workers. As a result, the public demanded a new law that would balance the rights of unions and the rights of employers.

This demand led to the Labor Management Relations Act of 1947, usually called the Taft-Hartley Act. It for the first time made certain union acts "unfair labor practices" and allowed employers to seek the aid of the national government to right them. Employers as well as workers could now present their cases before the National Labor Relations Board. A series of special rules was set up to handle strikes that in the opinion of the President might endanger the health or safety of the country. The President was given the power to forbid such strikes for eighty days while a special fact-finding committee appointed by him investigated the dispute.

54

At first, the unions violently opposed the Taft-Hartley Act because they were afraid it would destroy the power of organized labor. But time proved that the law was merely a check on the activities of the unions and one with which the unions could live. Rather than being injured by it, the unions seemed little affected and union membership continued to grow.

Later, perhaps partly as a result of the act, unions became aware of the need for greater regulation of internal union activities. As in all organizations, some members joined unions for purely selfish reasons. There were those who used illegal means to further their own interests, or who misused union funds. When such cases were publicly exposed, they gave unions a bad name. An intensive effort began to eliminate any possible Communist or criminal elements in unions, and as a result, in 1949–50, eleven unions were expelled from the CIO.

In 1953, two men who were to change the nature of the American labor movement were elected to offices in their unions: Walter Reuther became president of the CIO, and George Meany was named to head the AFL. Because both men believed strongly in labor unity, new efforts were made to reunite the two unions. After three years of discussion, an agreement for a merger was signed. A new union called the American Federation of Labor and Congress of Industrial Organizations was formed on December 5, 1955, and George Meany became president. This merger brought together under united leadership approximately 16 million workers, or between 85 and 90 percent of all union members in the United States.

During the first few years after the merger, public concern

AFL-CIO organizers Walter Reuther (1907–1970), left, and George Meany (1894–   ), two of labor's most prominent figures in the twentieth century. (AFL-CIO)

over possible corruption in unions continued. Two separate Senate committees investigated criminal influences on labor unions and partially as a result of the evidence they uncovered, three unions — the Teamsters, Bakery and Confectionery Workers, and Laundry Workers — were expelled from the AFL-CIO. New unions were organized by the AFL-CIO to recruit the members of the Bakery Workers and Laundry Workers who wanted to belong to a union in the AFL-CIO. The Teamsters, led by James Hoffa, became the largest United States union outside the AFL-CIO.

As a result of the Senate investigations, it was decided that laws were needed to protect union members. In 1959, the Labor-Management Reporting and Disclosure Act, commonly called the Landrum-Griffin Act, was passed. It is designed to protect the rights of the individual union members in their organizations. In fact, this

Organizer and first president of the Brotherhood of Sleeping Car Porters, A. Philip Randolph (1889–) became known for his work in both the labor and civil rights movements. (A. PHILIP RANDOLPH)

act is sometimes called labor's bill of rights. It also attempts to prevent any unfair or corrupt practices by unions.

In the years following the AFL-CIO merger, the United Auto Workers (UAW) became increasingly critical of the parent organization. Meany and Reuther no longer saw eye-to-eye on such problems as how to organize the unorganized, civil rights, foreign policy, and unemployment and poverty. Finally the UAW withdrew from the AFL-CIO. The Alliance for Labor Action was then created in July, 1968, with two of its charter members being the two largest unions in the country — the Teamsters and the UAW.

The labor movement in the United States is adding dramatic new pages to its history every day. There are major issues that need reexamination and solutions.

The Concern of Unions

Today, as unions have won their battle for recognition, and American society becomes more complicated and sophisticated, the issues surrounding modern unions have changed. Some of the problems that unions now face were unknown as recently as ten years ago. To understand the future of the union movement in the United States, we must briefly examine some of these new problems.

Automation

The problem of automation — the replacement of workers by complicated machines that do the same work in less time and at lower cost — has existed as long as man has attempted to use mechanical devices to aid him in his work. But the difficulty has become more complex with new strides in science and electronics and the arrival

A single operator puts an entire steel mill into operation through a fully automatic programmed system. (USWA)

of the computer age. It is the unions that must concern themselves with workers who are replaced by machines.

Unions and management make very careful agreements over the transition to the use of machines. It is usually gradual and involves a plan for retraining the displaced workers.

At present, most machines do the work of only unskilled workers, but as the machines become more complex, a growing number of skilled workers are affected. Unions must continue to seek new ways to deal with problems created by automation.

Right-to-Work Laws

Sometimes the public finds it hard to understand why unions insist on a *union-shop agreement* requiring all employees of a business to join the union. The union, however, feels that unless workers are compelled to join the union to hold their jobs, many workers will receive union benefits without assuming such responsibilities as paying union dues or observing union regulations. In situations where an employee can work without belonging to a union, the power of the union is greatly reduced. The union, therefore, usually tries to negotiate a union-shop agreement. In addition, the employer often agrees to a *dues checkoff* as part of the union-shop agreement. Then it becomes the job of the employer to deduct union dues automatically from the paychecks of the workers and to turn the money over to the union.

Many people feel that the union shop is contrary to basic American principles, because it forces a worker to join a union.

They also feel that an employer should be able to hire whomever he wants whether or not the worker is willing to join a union. In some states strong public opinion has led to the adoption of the so-called right-to-work laws, which make it illegal to compel any person to join a union in order to hold a job.

When the Taft-Hartley Act became law, one of its provisions called for an end to the traditional *closed shop* in any industry that came under federal jurisdiction. The closed shop agreement required employers to hire only those workers who already were union members in good standing.

There has been continuing public pressure for a national right-to-work law, while in states where right-to-work laws do exist, unions fight for their repeal. More than likely, the issue of right-to-work laws will continue to plague unions.

Closed Membership

Hiring through a union hiring hall allows a union to control membership and to engage in unfair practices with regard to the admission of apprentices.

The problems brought on by limiting union membership extend beyond labor-management relations. The unrestricted right to select new members results in union discrimination against members of minority groups, especially blacks and Puerto Ricans. Since not everyone is allowed to join a union, not everyone can work. Opponents of union control over hiring feel this is good enough reason to pass right-to-work laws.

Labor's support in an election can be important — and the candidates know it. Here, during the 1968 presidential campaign, Hubert Humphrey addresses New York garment workers. (ILGWU)

The Union and Politics

As the federal government becomes more important in our daily lives, unions tend to get more deeply involved in politics. However, it is doubtful whether unions will ever form a national labor party whose aim would be to seek union votes and secure union goals. Instead, unions will continue to support pro-labor candidates for public office — usually without regard to the candidates' political affiliations.

Naturally many unions maintain political lobbies in Washington to push for pro-labor legislation.

At the local level, candidates for political parties are supported openly if they are known to be friendly to labor. In addition, more labor activists are running for offices or joining the political world by serving on committees concerned with the entire population and not just unions.

Compulsory Arbitration

As both business and labor unions become larger and more powerful, some strikes affect more than a single locality. For example, a strike of airline machinists in 1966 stranded travelers all over the world and made air travel difficult everywhere in the United States.

In addition, there are some occupations involving public service where the right to strike is difficult to justify. Disaster can result when policemen, firemen, or sanitation workers go out on strike. Large numbers of government workers are joining unions:

64

over 2 million federal, state, and local employees are now union members. This is double the membership of ten years ago. During the postal employees' strike of 1970, we were able to see the havoc brought on by a strike of workers who provide an essential service.

Many Americans feel that the best way to avoid strikes affecting the public interest is compulsory arbitration. Briefly, this means that instead of a strike, the union and management are required to have a neutral third person or committee examine the situation. The union and management are compelled to accept the recommendations of the third party. Here again there is a dispute about fairness. In many cases, unions — and often management — feel that a third party does not have the special knowledge of the situation necessary to determine a proper solution. The union also opposes compulsory arbitration because it takes away the union's most powerful weapon — the right to strike.

With the increase of work stoppages involving essential services, the issue of compulsory arbitration will become even more pressing.

New Union Organization

During the past few years, union membership has remained at a relatively stable level and even — in many industries — shown a slight decline. Union membership has reached about 19 million according to the United States Department of Labor, Bureau of Statistics, but there are over 75 million people working in the United States. Although many of these workers could not easily fit into union organization, it does show that union membership could increase.

There are three areas where unions still do not have much power and membership: among white-collar, or office, workers; agricultural workers; and workers in the South.

Most white-collar workers have been reluctant to join a union because, among other things, they like to consider themselves part of management. The coming years will certainly see increased effort among unions to organize these kinds of workers. Perhaps the answer here is already taking shape — unaffiliated workers organizing themselves within their place of employment. These local groups band together — as factory workers did years ago — to present a united front to their employer. As the stratification between management and the employee becomes even more pronounced, belonging to a union does not mean the same thing it once did. Organization is no longer associated with the unionism that fought for recognition and came out of the roots of a rough and tumble world of workers. White-collar workers are beginning to see themselves as a group of people who must organize to receive fair treatment. Membership in unions in the white-collar areas is increasing and becoming a larger part of the total union membership.

Agricultural workers have always presented a problem for union organizers because they were so scattered and did not identify with the labor movement. Now, as farms become larger, unions are increasing their effort to establish effective locals of farm workers. This trend should continue and union representation will probably increase even though the total number of farm workers in the United States decreases as farming becomes more mechanized.

66

Cesar Chavez (far right) spent time and energy working, organizing, and negotiating to win recognition for his union and to gain fair treatment for its members. (AFL-CIO)

The migrant workers have been fighting for unionization. These workers, who travel from area to area to find work, have suffered greatly. Through the efforts of such leaders as Cesar Chavez, who gained a major victory for grape workers by providing a united front against growers, these workers are realizing the advantages of unionizing.

In the southern United States there is no strong tradition of great industry and union organization. However, as industry continues to move south, where land is available for factories, where taxes are more favorable, and where there is an available work force, unions are becoming more interested in organizing workers in this region. It is probable that in the future unions will become as strong and important in the South as they are elsewhere.

Blacks and Unionism

The discrimination toward blacks, which pervades United States society, seems common in labor unions. The construction unions stand out as being particularly offensive in this matter. Unions are most guilty of discrimination through closed membership and through establishing membership requirements that few blacks can meet.

National unions have tried to guide locals in establishing fair policies and have threatened to expel locals for carrying on discriminatory practices, but the locals seldom comply. In some cases a local union will eliminate discriminatory bylaws from its constitution but will continue the same practices as before. Even the

Steelworkers at a civil rights conference. Some unions still discriminate against black workers. (USWA)

AFL-CIO has had little success at the local level. There is little control over the activities of local or national unions that wish to discriminate against blacks and other minorities.

Perhaps only the federal government can end the racial imbalance of many unions. There already have been instances when federal funds were withheld from construction projects on which unions practiced segregation and discrimination. Unfortunately, the government has not yet realized that it will have to move more firmly and with more assurance to convince the unions that their members will lose work if government funds are cut off because of unjust union practices.

Women in the Labor Force

The first laws to be passed providing better hours and working conditions for workers affected women. In an irony of history, these laws sought to protect but also served to discriminate. Because women could work only a certain number of hours and at certain times, the maximum amount of pay they could earn was also limited. With the advent of the powerful women's liberation movement, women are pressing for rights equal to those of male workers. They are particularly interested in the equal pay for equal work statutes that have been passed at the national and state levels.

Today women are entering more industries than ever before. There are about four million women in unions and the number is increasing. As more women join the labor force, union membership grows.

A general membership meeting of the International Ladies' Garment Workers' Union, which traditionally has been made up of mostly female employees. (Local 23-25 ILGWU)

In addition, the increase in unionization among white-collar workers will be strengthened by women, who have traditionally held jobs as secretaries and clerks.

Equal pay for equal work can only be realized if women band together at a business or industry level to ensure fair treatment.

The Responsibility of Unions

A look at the role of labor unions in American life reveals that a union's activities are important to many more people than just union members. The way unions should and do act involves responsibilities to four different groups: to union members and their families, to industry and business, to government, and to consumers and the public. A union operates by maintaining a balance between the four.

The union's first responsibility is to its members. The goals pursued by the union reflect their desires. Years ago these goals were rather simple: better wages, better working conditions, and job security. Today they have grown more complex. The modern union on behalf of its members engages in activities that until recently never would have been considered part of the job of unions.

A union's responsibility to its members once stopped at the end of the workday or the worker's term of employment, but unions

73

today see their role as extending far beyond this point. More unions are developing programs to improve the lives of their older, retired members; these include recreational and cultural facilities. Some unions have built homes and even entire communities designed to house retired members. Some unions also sponsor educational programs devoted to union or political topics, while others move into the area of general education — often in cooperation with local high schools and colleges. Today it is not unusual for a union to conduct classes in American literature, public speaking, political history, or even stock-market investment. Many unions offer college and university scholarships for the children of members.

Most unions publish newspapers or magazines devoted to union activities. Ranging in size from a few pages to full-size, glossy magazines, they are designed to keep members in touch with the work of their union and the world around them. Some unions also sponsor radio and television programs on union views and activities.

Forward-looking unions are moving into such areas as counseling and vocational services, medical and dental care, and family recreational programs.

Progressive unions also acknowledge their responsibility to industry and business. Years ago unions felt that their job was simply to get as much as possible in wages and benefits for their members. Now they see the need to consider the financial health and special problems of the businesses with which they are bargaining. Unions realize that if they secure benefits for their members but weaken business they are not acting in their own best interests.

Many unions cooperate closely with management in seeking ways to increase the efficiency of their members by establishing

A weekend seminar allows union members to meet, learn, and relax (Local 23-25 ILGWU)

special training schools. Union economists and sociologists often join with representatives of management to plan for the future of an industry. Problems such as automation and plant location are regarded as union as well as management responsibilities.

Modern unions also recognize their responsibilities in the area of government. At the local level, unions encourage their members to register, vote, and take an interest in community affairs. Increasing numbers of union members are being elected or appointed to such governing bodies as school boards or city councils.

On the national level, unions are becoming more aware of their responsibility beyond specific union questions. They are concerned not only with special economic questions, but with much broader areas such as civil rights, education, and even foreign affairs. It is now common for the United States Congress or the President to seek the advice of labor leaders on national questions that do not directly involve unions. Many labor leaders serve on various government boards and committees as they recognize their increasing responsibilities in American life.

Finally, progressive modern unions realize they have a responsibility to consumers and the American public. The labor union movement in the United States has become powerful. In seeking to protect the well-being of their members and of the country, unions see how they must use their power in the interests of the American public as a whole and not confine their interests to a selfish gain.

Because increased wages and wage benefits often cause prices to rise, union leaders must take into account what their requests will ultimately do to the national economy.

Unions get out the vote. (AFL-CIO)

Striking grape workers in the West were supported by members as far away as New York City (Local 23-25 ILGWU)

Modern unions must realize the extent to which strikes and other work stoppages affect the public. Although many union members know that unions suffer in the long run when they gain a temporary advantage at the expense of the public, this is not always a prominent consideration when members of a union do strike.

In recent years, the unionization of government employees has grown rapidly. Other people are being organized in the areas that provide essential services: nurses, doctors, firemen, policemen. With strikes in these areas, the public will certainly be hurt. Can these strikes be justified? How will the unions handle work stoppages in these areas? How will the people respond? How will disputes be settled in these areas? Will the traditional last resort of the union — the strike — remain a part of the labor movement? These areas of unresolved problems are ones that will occupy unions, workers, and management for a long time to come.

Unionism in the United States has had a long and often troubled history. Today it faces old as well as new problems. It is because of the very flexibility of unionism in the past that it survives. If unions face up to today's problems with the same flexibility, they will continue to play an important role in American society.

Index

AFL-CIO (American Federation of Labor — Congress of Industrial Organizations), 12-13
creation of, 55-58
and discrimination, 70
UAW withdrawal from, 58
Agricultural workers, 66-67, 68
Alliance for Labor Action (1968), 13, 58
Amalgamated Association of Iron and Steel Workers, 11, 47
American Arbitration Association, 33-34
American Federation of Labor (AFL), 45-46
and CIO, 52-53, 55-58
American Railway Union, 47
Apprentices, 62
Arbitrator (arbitration), 25, 33-34
compulsory, 65
Assembly line, 40
Automation, 59-60, 76

Bakery and Confectionary Workers Union, 57
Benefit payments, 21
Blacks, 40-41, 62, 68-70
Bureau of Statistics (U.S. Dept. of Labor), 27, 65
Business agent, 9

Carnegie Steel Company, 47
Chavez, Cesar, 68
Child labor, 37, 50
Civil rights, 58, 76
Civil War (1861-65), 38
Clayton Anti-Trust Act (1914), 49
Closed shop, 62
Collective bargaining, 15, 23-25, 50
and grievance machinery, 29
history of, 35
legalized (1935), 51 (*see also* Wagner Act)
strikes as result of failure of, 25, 28 (*see also* Strikes)

81

ABOUT THE AUTHOR

Carolyn Sims was born and raised in Detroit, Michigan, a major city in terms of the American labor movement. Her interest in labor unions and their history developed early in her life. This interest was heightened at the University of Michigan, where she did both undergraduate and graduate work. While there, she had the good fortune to study under Professor William Haber, a prominent expert in labor relations and history. Ms. Sims lives in New York City, where she works for a major publishing company.